Healthy Thinking Habits

Seven Attitude Skills Simplified

Healthy Thinking Habits
Seven Attitude Skills Simplified

by
Cathy Burnham Martin

Quiet Thunder Publishing
Manchester, NH

www.QTPublishing.com

This title and more are featured in articles at
www.GoodLiving123.com.

Healthy Thinking Habits
Seven Attitude Skills Simplified

Copyright © 2015 Quiet Thunder Publishing
Manchester, NH

Paperback edition: ISBN 978-1-939220-06-6
Digital edition: ISBN 978-1-939220-07-3

Published and printed in the United States of America.

Library of Congress Control Number:
2015946122

ABOUT THE AUTHOR

Cathy Burnham Martin is a voiceover artist, journalist, corporate communications geek, and dedicated foodie. A former news anchor, she has written, produced, and hosted dozens of groundbreaking documentaries, TV specials, and news reports, ranging from the Moscow Super Power Summit and the opening of the Berlin Wall to extensive coverage of NH's First-in-the-Nation Presidential Primaries. Cathy also managed an award-winning community access TV station and writes articles for the acclaimed GoodLiving123.com blog. Her passion for great tasting, simple cooking led to the celebrated KISS™ Keep It Super Simple original recipe cookbook series.

A member of the Actors Equity Association, media coach, and business speaker, Cathy has been a Professional Member of the National Speakers Association since 1995. She attended Stetson University and graduated from Southern NH University. Enjoying adjunct faculty work, teaching persuasive public speaking and communications, Cathy earned a Master of Science in Corporate and Organizational Communications at Northeastern University in 2009. She also actively serves on boards for corporations and non-profits and was the 2009 recipient of Easter Seals' David P. Goodwin Lifetime Commitment Award.

OTHER TITLES

Additional writing credits include 300+ episodes of *New Hampshire Minutes,* plus being a contributing author in various books, including:
- **The Communication Coach: Business Communication Tips from the Pros** Jeffrey Tobe, Monroeville, PA
- **A Healthier You** Insight Publishing, Sevierville, TN

2007 saw the release of Cathy Burnham Martin's book, Dog Days in the Life of **The Miles-Mannered Man**, a whimsically philosophical collection of tall tales, wagging tails, and tantalizing treats, from Quiet Thunder Publishing, a division of SpeakEasy Corporate Communications in Manchester, NH.

This was followed by a number of other books, also from Quiet Thunder Publishing, including:

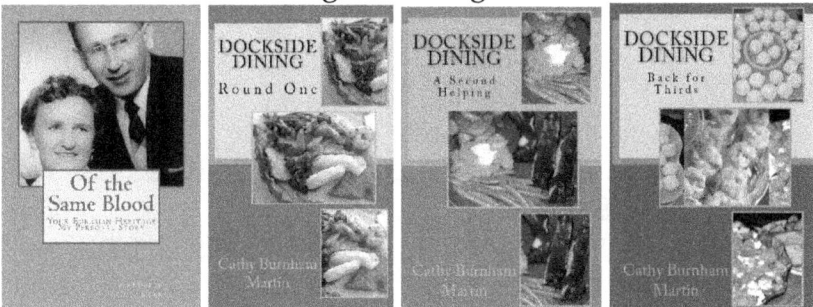

- **Of the Same Blood: Your Eurasian Heritage**
- **Dockside Dining: Round One**
- **Dockside Dining: A Second Helping**
- **Dockside Dining: Back for Thirds**

- **Cranberry Cooking**
- **Champagne: Facts, Fizz, Food & Fun**

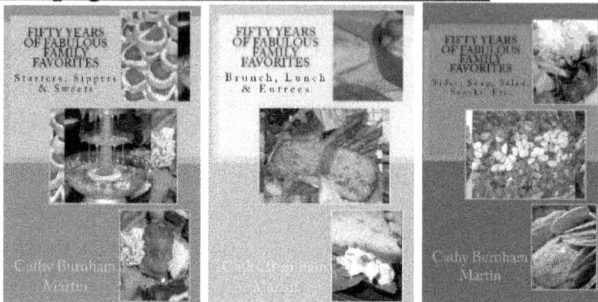

- **Fifty Years of Fabulous Family Favorites, Vols 1, 2 & 3**

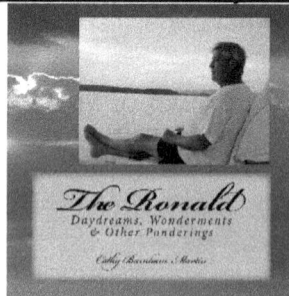

- **The Ronald: Daydreams, Wonderments, & Other Ponderings**
- **Sage, Thyme & Other Life Seasonings: Perspectives**

TABLE OF CONTENTS

INTRODUCTION

Most of us go through times of personal or professional doubt in our lives… Times when we don't think we seem to be able to do anything "right." Having spent my youth sporting one of the worst possible attitudes, sparked by inner turmoil, I successfully evolved into an extraordinarily positive adult. Here I share what a "Can Do" spirit can do for you and, more importantly, how you can make it your own.

Remarks made by celebrities, great thinkers, statesmen, and other individuals over the course of time play heavily in the way in which I illustrate my understanding of our attitudes and thinking. I think of these little gems as "Notable Quotables."

Healthy thinking is possible for all of us and gives us a great ability to become SASSY. Yes, I spell SASSY with all capital letters. My kind of SASS forms the acronym for Seven Attitude Skills Simplified. The "Y" stands for YOU because these skills can directly and wonderfully impact YOU and YOUR quality of life.

These seven skills are emPowerment, Planning, Perspective, Positive actions, Persistency, Poise, and Passion. And YOU are the reason for it all.

Standing on its own, Poise actually breaks down into what I call the 10 Confidence Commandments or Keys. They target posture, knowledge, character, initiative, cooperation, commitment, coolness under pressure, discipline, sportsmanship, and application.

I won't ramble through dozens of pages on each point. This guide is not about how many words I can spew. Wordiness tends to be much easier, as professional business speakers know. Writing a 1-hour speech takes far less time than a 10-minute speech. Still, I choose to be succinct, going straight to the heart of each point.

Just absorb and enjoy. Then personalize the Seven Attitude Skills Simplified to SASS up YOUR own life.

Chapter One
That's How the Trouble Began

"Eagles come in all shapes and sizes, but you will recognize them chiefly by their attitudes."
--Charles Prestwich Scott (1846-1932)
British newspaper editor

"You can make your bed with a smile, or you can make your bed with a frown, but you're going to make your bed." Those are words I heard often from my all-time Great American Mother, Glenna Burnham.

She had her hands full with my crummy childhood attitude, but a mere child was no match for this strong, determined woman! Sure she insisted on having a clean house, but she wanted happy, healthy children even more. My parents' multitude of lessons, once learned, would make me a far happier, healthier, and more resilient adult.

Medical experts agree that having a positive attitude means getting sick less often and, if sick, being able to recover quickly. Great attitudes are not easy to come by. What's even more annoying is the simple fact that we can't blame a bad attitude on genetics.

We can't control what happens to us or around us, but we have complete control over how we respond to it. That response can have an amazing impact on our health, both immediately and collectively.

Think about people with the uncanny ability to roll with the punches. Challenges seem to roll off their backs like water off a duck. Not everyone translates that outward sense of calm to inner peace. Looking smooth on the surface, but paddling like crazy underneath the water's surface could actually twist our stomach into knots or increase our risk of heart disease... all because of inner stress.

When impersonating Argentine actor Fernando Lamas, American entertainer and comedian Billy Crystal said, "*It's better to look good than to feel good, and you look mahhhvelous.*" But that was comedy; this is real life. Especially in the long run, we need to <u>feel</u> good in order to <u>look</u> good, and it all starts with how we think.

Healthy eating habits get plenty of attention. Healthy thinking habits should too. That means we need to develop good attitude habits, or healthy thinking habits, if you will.

We often hear that success is determined much more by attitude than aptitude or skill. Even the noted German physicist and genius, Albert Einstein, said, *"Imagination is more important than information."* Hmmm. I call that a ringing endorsement of the idea that attitude beats aptitude.

Generating a consistently great attitude is no small task. It's an ongoing process we need to maintain for the rest of our happy lives.

Our human tendency to resist things that are good for us reflects what I call that stubborn sassy streak of youth. As children we were taught not to sass, especially not to our elders. But, as Samuel Clemens, the 19th Century American humorist known as Mark Twain said, *"You should never 'sass' old people unless they 'sass' you first."*

The rules have changed. Take to heart the lessons offered here, and you'll have a new kind of SASS. This kind of SASS is not only okay, but it's a positively essential part of healthy living.

It may sound simple, and it can and will be, if you want. Again, SASS is simply my acronym for Seven Attitude Skills Simplified. You can truly call them the "P" vitamins. Remember, the seven skills are emPowerment, Planning, Perspective, Positive actions, Persistency, Poise, and Passion. A minimum daily "P" vitamin requirement may not have yet been established, but a healthy and happy, quality life most certainly needs all seven. Their benefits are cumulative, but daily supplements of each are beneficial.

Chapter 2
SASS #1: emPowerment

"Only I can change my life. No one can do it for me."
--Carol Burnett (1933 -)
American actress and comedian

All too often, people look outside themselves for happiness… for empowerment… for someone else to make sense of all the nonsense. Yet, we each have complete control over our own attitudes and happiness. Your good or bad attitude is _someone's_ decision – let's make it <u>yours</u>.

Why *do* people feel powerless so often? It's been said that if you think you are too small to be effective, you have never been in the dark with a mosquito. (A smile with a little perspective helps.) Throughout the ages, many great minds have commented on our ability to choose how we feel about life and who we are.

- Roman philosopher Seneca (4 BC – 65 AD) -- *"A man is as unhappy as he has convinced himself he is."*

- United States First Lady Eleanor Roosevelt (1884 – 1962) -- *"No one can make you feel inferior without your consent. Never give it to them."*

- Writer and humorist Mark Twain (1835-1910) -- *"The worst loneliness is not to be comfortable with yourself."*

Empowering yourself means believing in yourself and being the person you want people to know you are. This does <u>not</u> mean being perfect. Making no mistakes is NO blessing. The fact that it's not possible anyway is AOK, because we can <u>*correct*</u> most mistakes. That's why pencils have erasers. Remember the adage that anything worth doing is worth doing poorly, until we can learn to do it well. So, step out boldly.

Another key to boosting personal power is to do what <u>you</u> expect of yourself, rather than what others may expect of you or what you may *think* they expect of you. That's a biggie. We tend to get so wrapped up in trying to please other people that we can get to the point where we're less able to please anyone. If that sounds familiar, STOP. Let it go. If you really want to be able to treat other people fantastically then you must be able to start with yourself. Please place yourself prominently on your priority list.

When we lose that balance we lose perspective. We get stressed.

Remember all the talk about "middle child syndrome?" I lived that angst of overcompensating to try and please everyone. I was sad and felt very alone. I worked crazily to do everything well. Though a classic overachiever, I regularly felt I wasn't doing enough. In reality, I had NO reason to feel that way, but I'd bought into a rather self-destructive philosophy. It took years for me to figure it out, but, in truth, no one liked me more or less if I did or did not do a multitude of things.

By my pre-teen years, my father compared me and my attitude swings to a clock's pendulum that was out of balance. He said my emotional swings needed moderation if I wanted to find happiness. Very correctly he observed that when I was "up" no one could be higher. I was a delight and full of positive energy. But when I was "down" no one could be lower. I was as miserable an adolescent as anyone could hope to never meet. Dad suggested that I think about it and see if life wasn't happier if I could get that personal pendulum to moderate in the middle.

Then I slumped into guilt, thinking that I'd actually disappointed everyone I loved. I felt that I'd let people down by working so very hard to do things that I thought would please them. These were my feelings... my thoughts.

Downward spirals are fast and furious. They may not be logical, but when you are living them, they <u>are</u> reality. What we struggle to realize is that they don't have to <u>stay</u> as our reality.

We need to forgive ourselves for being human. We need to think logically to get a better foundation, and we need honest emotion to give us true commitment and warmth.

Balance helps us to open a window in our self-created dark place and let in some light. Only then have we given ourselves the power to grow and develop.

Some people call it reinventing yourself. I call it emPowering you. Call it anything you like; just do it.

Chapter 3
SASS #2: Planning

"Hope for the best, but prepare for the worst."
\--English proverb

Until it's a habit, planning is often easier said than done. The point, however, is undeniable.

Plan. Give your days, years, and life some clear direction and targets. Set goals.

Determine specific steps needed to reach your goals. Realize that setbacks and detours along the way are natural.

It seems realistic that we don't plan to fail. Failure usually comes because we failed to plan. But planning is a learned skill. Many of us never quite master day-to-day time management, never mind long-term goal setting.

One key is taking charge of that daily Must Do list. Of course, that means we should create lists in the first place.

I know people who never write down appointments. They don't carry a calendar, and why should they? In all seriousness, they'd never look at it anyway.

However, these same people get anxious when they suddenly realize they're late for a commitment or have missed something altogether. Or they make other plans and get upset when time conflicts cause angst. They feel frustrated and exhausted much of the time.

That's unfortunate, since it's totally avoidable. We can control our windows of time far more than we may think.

There are many things we <u>can't</u> control in our lives. Why miss out on something simple that <u>gives</u> us control? Maintaining a daily, weekly, monthly, and annual calendar lets us plan ahead, keep buffer time between events, block out personal time and accommodate family commitments. We keep control and relieve the pressure of panic and rushing.

When we follow a schedule we can make adjustments that work <u>for</u> us. We can actually fit more into a day and end up accomplishing much more, too.

Keeping a calendar up to date is easier now than ever, especially considering all the electronic gadgets most of us carry. In fact, a multitude of free cell phone applications can keep track of appointments and even remind you as they approach.

New York and North Carolina entrepreneur Dexter Yager often said, *"True dreams are goals with dates. The rest are just wishes."* So, a little planning can go a long way.

Consider these simple, yet specific action steps:

- Write down big and little goals.

- Identify small steps required to accomplish each goal.

- Do the needed tasks to follow the success steps that you've identified.

- Set deadlines for yourself. Even jazz pianist and composer Duke Ellington (1899-1974) said, *"I don't need time. What I need is a deadline."*

- Put needed action items in your calendar with blocked out time for each.

- Prioritize your short- and long-term, daily, and lifetime goals.
- Be very specific. "I will try twelve new restaurants

within the next twelve months" is better than "I want to find some new places to eat."

- If visual reminders help you stay focused, cut out representative photos or encouraging words, and pin them places where you'll see them.

- Consider where and when you are most apt to get off track and build up defenses <u>now</u> to be ready to fight back <u>then</u>.

- Be sure your goals are truly <u>yours</u> and not someone else's goals for you.

- Be realistic. Don't overwhelm yourself. The best way to eat an elephant is one bite at a time.

- When you stumble, get back up and start trying again.

- Believe you will win!

Now, is goal setting really that important? Yes. Plain and simple. **Forbes** magazine founder, B.C. Forbes, said, *"If you don't drive your business, you'll be driven out of business."*

That applies to life. Those who cannot or will not discipline themselves are destined to be disciplined by others. Control your time or others will control it. We've usually heard such lines before, because they're true. We must not wait for the right circumstances or day or mood. The stars typically do not line up perfectly for our every whim. It matters not. Decide that today is yours and move forward.

We never want to just let life happen to us. We'd only end up feeling out of control. Kahlil Gibran, the 20th Century mystic philosopher, said, *"We choose our joys and sorrows long before we experience them."* So, set positive goals and then work to make achieving them your reality.

Chapter 4
SASS #3: Perspective

"Whether you think you can or think you can't,
you're usually right."
--Henry Ford (1863 – 1947)
American industrialist and Ford Motor Company founder

Whenever we think we're being objective, we should probably think again. True objectivity is an ideal, but it's very difficult in our day-to-day living. As humans, we tend to develop and then hold extremely rigid views and opinions.

Our innate stubbornness can actually inspire sadness and doubt. We just "hope" we are right. Even when we loudly advocate our position, nagging doubts often chip away at our confidence.

When we learn we've been wrong, we respond. We choose our response either openly or subconsciously. Sometimes we rationalize the facts so that we can justify what we'd believed so strongly was true. That can appear to be a more palatable solution than stepping up to the plate and admitting we were off in our thinking.

We can actually refuse to shift our perspective because we don't want to admit we were wrong. We may truly struggle with the concept that we have anything to "learn." We may puff up and rant and rave, even though that only reveals our stubborn, ignorant, and intolerant side. In truth, these rationalizations deteriorate our self-respect and step heavily on our chances for a consistently good attitude.

Sometimes, as we develop wisdom, we can shift to recognize a view that we hadn't previously had room for in our minds. We accept new facts and open our perspective. We can do this graciously and "eat a little crow," if need be. Humbling ourselves and accepting we are human enables us to grow and learn comfortably.

Permitting ourselves to be enlightened is very healthy. It relieves frustration, lets us laugh at ourselves, and helps us understand others. Laughing at ourselves is particularly important, because it's far too easy to take ourselves too seriously.

I really like the perspective from French writer Nicholas Chamfort (1741 – 1794). *"Swallow a toad in the morning and you will encounter nothing more disgusting the rest of the day."* Now <u>there's</u> some food for thought – very "punny," I know. Sorry about that.

Allowing new evidence or thinking to change or upgrade our perspective also means that in future situations we are more likely to be more open minded... to think more calmly and objectively.

This lowers stress levels considerably and thus helps us stay healthier. Consider the words of American author and philosopher, Henry David Thoreau (1817 – 1862). *"It's not what you look at that matters, it's what you see."*

We grow when we see the full spectrum of Life. None of us is so swift or brilliant that we cannot grow by seeing things differently, from a new perspective. It teaches us to live with a positive and gentle sense of humility. We are not in Life alone. We do not achieve greatness alone.

For me, humility was an unexpected, but important perspective gained early as a TV broadcaster. There's no escaping the true strength of the human spirit.

- I reported on the sad path of very ill children with timeless souls and unending love, and I marveled at their faithful courage.

- Behind the iron curtain in Moscow, KGB-hounded people shared their nightmare, real-life stories with the most amazing combination of hope and desperation. I was moved beyond words. I've never before felt so powerless, angry, sad, and fortunate all at the same time.

- When nervously anxious East Germans boldly stepped through the small, early openings in the Berlin Wall in 1989 into the little oasis of freedom called West Berlin, I was immediately humbled into tears by the multitudes of grateful hugs I received. Though undeserving of their outpourings, I was seen as representative of all that the United States of America and our Allies had done to keep hope alive and secure their chance to be free after decades of oppression. Humbling indeed, especially when you think about all the people who had suffered and died.

We all need good doses of perspective. We grow when we allow people to touch us and open our eyes. US President Franklin D. Roosevelt (1882 – 1945) understood perspective clearly when he said, *"The only limit to our realization of tomorrow will be our doubts of today."*

Eleanor Roosevelt, his First Lady as he served from 1933 to 1945, knew how to put perspective into action. She reminded us that, *"A stumbling block to the pessimist is a stepping stone to the optimist."*

I like that perspective very much. We can't eliminate challenges, but we can learn to see the possibilities and likelihood, rather than the impossibilities and improbabilities. Now *that* is a good kind of SASSY.

Chapter 5
SASS #4: Positive Actions

> *"The reason why worry kills more people than work*
> *is that more people worry than work."*
> --Robert Frost American poet
> Pulitzer Prize in 1923, '24, '30, '36, & '42

Having knowledge but not applying it is like begging for unrealized potential. American humorist Will Rogers (1879 – 1935) said, *"Even if you're on the right track, you'll get run over if you just sit there."* That's true, but not just any action will suffice.

For example, if you row a boat really hard with just one oar in the water, you might go really fast but only in circles. Activity alone doesn't get the job done nor relieve your stress. You need to take the _right_ action.

That means actually <u>doing</u> what you know you should do. And yet, when we do things in our lives that <u>don't</u> generate the desired results, why do we often continue to do those same things?

Remember the American televangelist Robert H. Schuller (1926 – 2015)? I liked his recognition of this human foible, *"It takes guts to get out of the ruts."*

20th century physicist and creator of the theory of relativity, Albert Einstein, said, *"The definition of insanity is doing the same thing over and over again and expecting a different result."*

That's like cartoon character Charlie Brown banging his head against a tree to make the tree grow faster. Of course, it does not. You've likely heard the old line that we're banging our head against the tree because it feels so good when we stop! What we miss sometimes is the great lesson: Don't do it again. Then we can avoid the pain completely.

As humans, it's our birthright to live and learn. Experience is the best teacher, but that's especially true when we can learn from someone *else's* experience. Our human stubborn streak often restricts our ability to accept someone else's advice. A "wet paint" sign is meaningless; we have to prove to ourselves that the paint on the bench really is wet. The results? We wear a little paint.

Take positive action steps:

- Find activities that yield positive results; repeat them.

- Recognize activities that drain personal resources – energy, time, attitude, and finances; avoid them.

- Polish skills that support positive activities.

- Practice. Practice. Practice.

- Don't give up if not skillful at first.

Long before he was famous, the great French sculptor Auguste Rodin (1840 – 1917) recognized, *"Nothing is a waste of time if you use the experience wisely."*

If you are in or desire a position of leadership, you also need to recognize an additional responsibility. People follow based on trust and respect. It would be great if all managers had leadership skills. Sadly, we all know managers who are in those roles due to promotions, not leadership ability. We try to understand those people, but we certainly don't want to emulate them or be anything like them.

In any role in life, we can be happier and healthier if we honestly adopt leadership skills. This means doing things like:

- Setting the right example

- Supporting other people's efforts

- Delegating all possible activities

- Trusting other people's talents and intentions

- Following through

- Recognizing and rewarding others' accomplishments

- Not procrastinating

- Respecting other people's time

- Practicing good time management

I also like to give credit to others for everything that goes well, while accepting responsibility for things that don't. This helps people trust us and inspires them to work harder for positive results... *without* fears of failure or unnecessary pressure.

It's so easy to get busily caught up in a false, self-inflicted straightjacket of stress in which we put the world and its woes squarely on our own shoulders. Set yourself free and help others do the same by getting your own act together.

Some may think that following lists and schedules is too restrictive to our sense of freedom. Well, remember, you can take a train off its tracks. It is then free, but it can't go anywhere. Tracks exist for a very good reason.

So, lay out some tracks for yourself. Make a schedule as one of your priorities.

- Review and update your day's plan each morning.

- Post reminders wherever you need to, until following your schedule becomes a habit.

- Stay on course. If you have five things that must be accomplished, don't let yourself get off track, doing items 6-10.

- Maintain control over your time. Get the "must do" items done first.

Steps such as these lower stress and actually provide more time to accomplish additional items on your "Must Do" list and even your "Should Do" and your "Wish To Do" lists.

Perhaps most important to your good health, especially if you tend toward Type A personality traits, is to let the day come to an end. Walk out the door. Don't take work home with you. We all need to refresh and recharge. It will all still be there the next day. Live your life in such a way that there just isn't a chance for burning out.

That is part of self-respect.

Another wonderfully refreshing thing happens when you are taking the right actions. You prove nay-sayers wrong.

There are always those people wringing their hands and groaning about their failures as if always caused by other people or circumstances beyond their control. They rant about why things can't be done. Hah! People actually doing those very things repeatedly interrupt the naysayers! *That* is not only fun, but also it makes the discipline and effort of doing the right things even more satisfying and personally rewarding.

Regardless of who you are, I add one other, rather specific positive action to the "Must Do" list. That is play.

As children, we did this naturally. As we grew into adulthood, most of us were weaned off playing. That's sad.

We need to learn to play again and be sure to allow ourselves some regular playtime. It doesn't matter what you love to do. Just do it. Have fun. Laugh out loud – often. Enjoy this time called Life.

"We do not stop playing because we grow old. We grow old because we stop playing!"

--Benjamin Franklin
18th Century US statesman, writer & scientist

Chapter 6
SASS #5: Persistency

"I'm a great believer in luck.
The harder I work, the more I have of it."
--Thomas Jefferson (1743 – 1826)
3rd US President; crafter of the Declaration of Independence

The truth about being persistent is plain and simple... it works. Persistency gets the job done. We only get flustered when we stop short of our goal. We plan and prepare for a particular project as a three-hour task. Perhaps it turns out to be a five-hour task. We can't win if we give up after four hours.

The adage is true that says, *"A big shot is just a little shot that kept on shooting."* We can't win if we give up and don't keep trying until we get the job done. Movie fans of the "Star Wars" films remember the fictional Jedi Master Yoda's sage remark, *"Do or do not. There is no try."*

So much has been written and said about being persistent and consistent. In all walks of life it is seen as key to success, self-image, and accomplishment. It doesn't matter whether we're trying to learn to make a good pasta sauce or master a new computer software program.

In a typical yo-yo dieting pattern, we may discipline ourselves to lose an extra five, ten, or even twenty pounds. Then we celebrate by returning to old habits till every pound returns. Why? We failed to develop a positive, persistent action plan. Honestly, can you think of any skill or endeavor that is not improved by a dedicated, persistent effort?

Hollywood movie mogul Cecil B. DeMille (1881 – 1959) said, "*The person who makes a success of living is the one who sees his goal steadily and aims for it unswervingly. That is dedication.*"

Author and motivator Zig Ziglar (1926 – 2012) noted, "*Others can stop you temporarily… YOU are the only one who can do it permanently.*"

And no matter how great a champion you are, the need for persistence doesn't waiver. Consider the words of the great Jewish-American composer Irving Berlin (1888 – 1989), "*The toughest thing about success is that you've got to keep on being a success.*"

The awareness of persistence as a major key has been clear for centuries. 20th Century American basketball coach Pat Riley (born in 1945) recognized the vital role of persistence with his words, *"Excellence is the gradual result of always striving to do better."*

We note that such thinking is hardly a new concept, since 4th Century Greek philosopher Aristotle (385 BC – 322 BC) wrote, *"We are what we repeatedly do. Excellence, therefore, is not an act but a habit."*

The simplicity is having a goal that's important enough to you that you'll persist in the effort needed. How will this make you healthier, you may ask? A stagnant pool of water has no sparkle. We are brightest when we are moving… moving toward something that matters to us. Making an effort once, even if successful, is good but less fulfilling than working steadily to improve.

My mother didn't bake the best pies in town on her first attempt. In fact, when she married my father she said that she couldn't cook at all, never mind bake. He taught her the basics, and the rest is history. Her pies became the consistently closest thing to perfection imaginable. I never again expect to find a crust that is lighter, flakier, or more melt-in-your-mouth delicious than Mom's. Nor am I apt to ever taste fillings that are any fresher, juicier, or so carefully spiced to accentuate natural flavors. She gained undisputed Best Cook in Town status through her persistence.

When I hear someone moaning and groaning about their lack of talent or luck or skill, I know better. They just haven't tried hard enough or persisted long enough.

Think of a tennis match. The pros launch these rocket-propelled ace serves right past their opponents. Do they land these every time? No, but consistently ace-quality serves are surely their goal. They practice their serve hundreds of times each week.

They are not trying to best the 99.9% of the population they could beat without such practice. They are persistent so they can be their very best when they face a like-minded professional. The best in their sports want to beat the best, fair and square, with their hard-earned and persistently-honed skills. Winning by mere default is a hollow victory.

There comes great fulfillment and satisfaction for all of us when our persistence pays off with consistent quality. Someone can easily have better raw talent than you do in some area. However, you can zoom past them if you are persistent in the necessary work to improve... or they allow their skills to falter or stagnate. Persistence. Don't take your eyes off the ball.

The simple truth is based on simple facts. We succeed when we are willing to do what it takes... over and over again.

Chapter 7
SASS #6: Poise

"Somehow I can't believe there are many heights
that can't be scaled by a man
who knows the secret of making dreams come true.
This special secret can be summarized in four C's.
They are: curiosity, confidence, courage, and constancy,
and the greatest of these is confidence."
                              --Walt Disney (1901-1966)
                              American entrepreneur and cartoonist

Poise is a very multi-faceted skill, and it definitely shines from the inside out. When someone is particularly poised, they exude confidence. Poise is never pompous; it is classy. Someone who is poised has magnetism, pizzazz, chutzpah. A poised person truly lives what I call the Ten Confidence Commandments or Keys.

1. **Physical** -- Maintain a physical posture and clean presentation to exude a magnetic aura and positive air. As 21st Century New York cartoonist Marty Bucella says, *"When it comes to staying young, a mind-lift beats a face-lift any day."*

2. **Initiative** – If you want a competitive advantage in life, demonstrate the foresight of initiative. You have a good idea? Go for it. On this point I defer to New Zealand author Lloyd Jones, born in 1955, who said, *"Those who try to do something and fail are infinitely better than those who try to do nothing and succeed."*

3. **Character** – Be of strong character, built on integrity, trustworthiness and selflessness. Do all you can to squelch sarcasm, cockiness and shallow airs of superiority. Be the person we want other people to believe we are. In the words of American essayist, Ralph Waldo Emerson, *"What lies behind us and what lies before us are tiny matters compared to what lies within us."*

4. **Knowledge** – Keep knowledge as your foundation, preparing well and honing skills. However, as we practice life-long learning, never accept ignorance in yourself, but do tolerate it in others. 3rd Century Greek biographer Diogenes Laërtius wrote, *"Confidence, like art, never comes from having all the answers; it comes from being open to all the questions."*

5. **Commitment** – Do whatever it takes. Give whatever you can. With full commitment, you can live well with yourself, regardless of the results. Italian artist and inventor Leonardo da Vinci lived from 1452 till 1519. He noted, *"Obstacles cannot crush me. Every obstacle yields to stern resolve. He who is fixed to a star does not change his mind."*

6. **Steadiness** – Keep cool under pressure. Don't waver from what is right. Stay the course. During the birth of the United States, American philosopher Thomas Paine (1737-1809) is noted for saying, *"I love men who can smile in trouble, who can gather strength from distress, and grow brave by reflection."*

7. **Teamwork** – Be a cooperative believer in and practitioner of teamwork. Surround yourself with positive people. Choose supportive friends, not destructive or complacent associates for your inner circle or team. NFL football coach George H. Allen (1922-1990) said, *"Football isn't necessarily won by the best players. It's won by the team with the best attitude."*

8. **Expectation** – Live with great expectation and positive
    anticipation of what you want and what you hope to gain.
    Claim the positive. In his book <u>Seeds of Greatness</u>, Denis
    Waitley, born in 1933, wrote, *"Life is a self-fulfilling prophecy:
    You won't necessarily get what you want in life, but in the long
    run, you <u>will</u> usually get what you expect."*

9. **Perseverance** – Discipline yourself to hang in there to
    overcome struggles and challenges. British Prime Minister
    Sir Winston Churchill (1874 – 1965) said, *"Courage is going
    from failure to failure without losing enthusiasm."*

10. **Sportsmanship** – Become a Morale Booster Extraordinaire.
    Lift others up and celebrate their hard-earned successes.
    Win by achieving. Respect the achievements of others.
    Novelist Edith Wharton (1862-1937) shared words on this
    that are precious. *"There are two ways of spreading light: to be
    the candle or the mirror that reflects it."*

        With true confidence, we possess that elusive quality
called poise. Because confidence-building skills are all learned
from the inside out, anyone can have this powerful poise. The
more poised a person is, the healthier they tend to be also.

Chapter 8

SASS #7: Passion

"There is no greatness without a passion to be great."
-- Ralph Waldo Emerson (1803-1882)
American writer & philosopher

The premise and promise of passion in success has been bantered about and debated for generations. Some devotees to pure logic tend to resist the thought of enthusiasm or anything emotional having a positive influence. For me, the enthusiasm of passion is the simple key to attitude beating aptitude.

Consider **Candidate A** versus **Candidate B**:

Candidate A possesses basic skills and little experience.
Candidate B brings top skills and great experience.

A has sparkle in the eyes and high energy. **B** shows distrust in the eyes and has a slouching posture, appearing unsure.

Candidate A engages in positive conversation, with a bright and genuine smile. **Candidate B** is a classic naysayer, with a terse, all-business expression.

Healthy Thinking Habits

Candidate A seeks and sees the good in situations and possesses a wonderful sense of humor. **Candidate B** thinks positive thinkers are pushovers and offers polite laughter at best.

A accepts change as growth potential and faces life with an even and upbeat mood. **B** resists change as a threat and delivers brooding, changeable moods.

Candidate A is thoughtful, open and honest, makes people feel relaxed, and lifts other people up. **Candidate B** is insensitive, guarded and careful, generates tension in others, and walks on people.

It's your choice. It doesn't matter if you're considering a politician, friend, co-worker, committee member, employee, or boss, **Candidate A** is far more enthusiastic than **Candidate B**. **Candidate A** can be trained for needed skills and gain the experience. Though **Candidate B** brings skills, it's pretty tough to train for attitude or enthusiasm.

Candidate A shows respect for other people and seems open to growth. **Candidate B** feels superior and lets people know it. Which one would you want on your team? On *any* team?

Both enthusiasm and misery are extremely contagious. The choice is yours as to how you will infect your world. In truth, some rather powerfully successful people and logical thinkers have <u>insisted</u> on enthusiasm being key in life.

- Henry Ford – *"You can do anything if you have enthusiasm. Enthusiasts are fighters, they have fortitude; they have staying qualities. Enthusiasm is at the bottom of all progress! With it, there is accomplishment. Without it there are only alibis."*

- American football coach Vince Lombardi (1913-1970) – *"If you aren't fired with enthusiasm, you will be fired with enthusiasm."*

- Business tycoon Malcolm Forbes (1919 – 1990) – *"Men who never get carried away should be."*

- Albert Einstein – *"There are only two ways to live your life. One is as though nothing is a miracle. The other is as though everything is a miracle."*

Life is truly a matter of how we choose to look at it. Consider the following fact. The same negative circumstances can be applied to two different people with dramatically different results. Why? Because we have free will, we can each choose how we'll react. We can tremble and stay a victim. We can point fingers and blame people or circumstances for our woes. Or we can learn new strengths and wisdom and move ahead.

For some perspective on looking at life with passion, consider:

- American activist Helen Keller (1880 – 1968) -- *"Life is either a daring adventure, or nothing."*

- Italian-American racing champion Mario Andretti, born in 1940 -- *"If everything's under control, you're going too slow."*

- Mark Twain – *"It's not the size of the dog in the fight, it's the size of the fight in the dog."*

- US Attorney General Robert F. Kennedy (1925 – 1968) -- *"Only those who dare to fail greatly can ever achieve greatly."*

- American tennis champion, born in 1943, Billie Jean King -- *"Be bold. If you're going to make an error, make a doozy, and don't be afraid to hit the ball."*

- Walt Disney – *"It's kind of fun to do the impossible."*

Chapter 9
Happy Living

Developing SASS, the Seven Attitude Skills Simplified, means being sassy in all the right ways. We're here on Earth too briefly, as it is. SASS up your life. Start thinking healthier.

A happy, healthy life is not the result of meek thinking. Live boldly. US President Lyndon Baines Johnson (1908 – 1973) said, *"I'd rather give my life than be afraid to give it."* That rings clearly with patriotism. My variation reflects the need to live with passion and life fully. I like to say, *"I'd rather truly live my life than be afraid to live it."*

On top of the spirit of adventure in our passion for daily living, we should also add a large helping of humor. No other single tool is more valuable in our quest to live well. People who scowl don't get to enjoy the healing power of humor. It reflects the old saying, *"Growl all day and you'll feel dog-tired all night."* It's a simple fact that an upbeat attitude helps make light work of any task.

Our health benefits greatly when we add laughter. That's why a good comedian is so refreshing. Day-to-day living can be highly stressful. Turn on the TV news or tune into any news site online, and you'll see our human dark side at work. Life's miseries are displayed boldly and repeatedly, because bad news draws us in. Our attitude and health both suffer if we forget that it's just another program fighting for a share of the splintering market share. They don't typically report on the 99.9% of what's going on that is wonderful.

Positive events fill the vast majority of real life… people helping people, community successes, kids who are not stealing cars or overdosing on drugs, politicians who are not cheating or stealing, safe and productive schools, honest businesses, and enthusiastic volunteers, working to boost other people's quality of life. This does not mean donning rose-colored glasses or pretending life is beautiful all the time. It is not. However, healthy happiness requires perspective.

Oscar-winning actress Katharine Hepburn (1907 – 2003) shared good advice for this. She said, *"Life can be wildly tragic at times, and I've had my share. But whatever happens to you, you have to keep a slightly comic attitude. In the final analysis, you have got not to forget to laugh."*

We do need humor to get through challenges. A good belly laugh is a healthy thinking cornerstone. As American comedian Flip Wilson (1933-1998) put it, *"Funny is an attitude."* We do need to exercise our attitudes just as we should exercise our bodies. Editor Norman Cousins (1915-1990) saw the impact of humor and said, *"Laughter is inner jogging."*

It's all a matter of choice. In the same way that we choose to be a good or bad role model, we choose to have a good or bad attitude. Choosing the positive boosts our success, happiness, and health immeasurably.

In SASS #1, I told you about my father's pendulum example as he tried to teach me moderation. Because I was a brat, I stubbornly defied what I recognized as good advice. Quietly, however, it made sense to me. Though my resistant self would let me do *exactly* as my Poppy advised, I still chose to work persistently on creating a moderate swing in the *upper*, more positive mood area. Sure enough, I very gradually learned how to be a happier person every day.

Now, this was not an overnight transformation by any means, but it worked. Decades later I still moderate in that upper range. If I'm having a "bad day," my husband asks that I please tell him. And my "bad days" tend to last for a couple of hours. Talk about a 180-degree turn-around!

I recall a day in the mid-1980's when I read an article in "USA Today" that noted "less than 2% of Americans wake up happy." I was truly taken aback. I had sensed that I was "different," but I hadn't realized just *how* different. I don't ever need a cup of coffee to get in step with the morning; I wake up ready to roll. Better health? Absolutely. Higher resiliency? Unquestionably.

There's another exciting benefit to the power and purpose that positive passion brings to life. Youthful vitality. Though I'm "of a certain age" at the time of this writing, people tend to be very surprised if they learn my age, erroneously tagging me for 10, 15, and even 20 years younger.

I've always presumed that I've looked my age at every age. Both friends and strangers correct me regularly. This is not attributable to a great diet or stress-free living, I can assure you. I believe a great attitude, centered around a true passion for living and a strong faith in God makes all the difference.

If I'm feeling "down," I not only feel slow and low, but the mirror reflects a face that looks tired and so much older! I see my sallow complexion, no sparkle or vitality in my eyes, an expressionless mouth. Eek! Who is that?!? My exterior reflects what's inside. Low enthusiasm shows. This tends to ring true for all of us.

To me, enthusiasm _is_ passion. People with positive passion for life both appear and feel more vigorous and healthier – at every age.

I sum up the simplicity of the skill of passion with the legendary words of Watterson Lowe, "_Years may wrinkle the face, but to give up enthusiasm wrinkles the soul._" Before this book, you may well have already had a gleefully wrinkle-free soul. If so, that's awesome. If not so much, that's okay, too.

Regardless of where you are starting, with the Seven Attitude Skills Simplified, you're well on your way to reducing stress and loading your life with control, quality, and even more enthusiasm. These "P" vitamins definitely keep our attitudes healthy too. Put a little SASS in your life and enjoy a healthier you.

For more information,

free articles, and publications from

Cathy Burnham Martin,

check out her blog articles and archives

on the

www.GoodLiving123.com website.

www.ingramcontent.com/pod-product-compliance
Lightning Source LLC
Chambersburg PA
CBHW071936020426
42331CB00010B/2896